flea market fidos

flea market fidos

the dish on dog junk
and canine collectibles

barri leiner and marie moss

stewart, tabori & chang
new york

for emma and maisy

for emma and maisy

Published in 2002 by
STEWART, TABORI & CHANG
A Company of La Martinière Groupe
115 West 18th Street, New York, NY 10011

Export Sales to all countries except
Canada, France, and French-speaking
Switzerland:
Thames and Hudson Ltd.
181A High Holborn
London WC1V 7QX
England

Canadian Distribution:
Canadian Manda Group
One Atlantic Avenue, Suite 105
Toronto, Ontario M6K 3E7
Canada

Library of Congress Cataloging-in-Publication Data

Leiner, Barri.
    Flea market fidos : the dish on dog junk and canine collectibles /Barri Leiner and
    Marie Moss.
        p. cm.
    ISBN 1-58479-253-1
        1. Dogs--Collectibles--United States. I. Marie Moss. II. Title.

NK4891.2 .L45 2002
636.7--dc21

2002021239

Printed in Hong Kong

10 9 8 7 6 5 4 3 2 1

First Printing

design by nicole salzano and nancy kruger cohen
still photography by aimée herring

contents

A pair of pals take
in the sights at
the Kane County
Fairgrounds in Illinois.

intro

we love junk and everything about it. From dollar bill discoveries to discovering the real McCoy, our lives are overflowing with coveted collectibles. Not a day goes by that we are not planning our next junking journey, reveling in yesterday's yard sale finds, or dreaming of the next what-will-we-find search for hidden treasure.

We caught the junking bug years ago and have never searched for a cure. Whether we are checking road maps and directions or packing up a sturdy backpack, the shared anticipation of a junking day can't be beat. After all, where else can girlfriends stomp around muddy fairgrounds, share conversation and French fries and uncover one-of-a-kind flea finds. We have seen treasure hiding beneath the heaps, bins and booths of many a flea market, roadside stop and yard sale and along the way we have discovered the kind of friendship that can't be bought or bargained for.

Our treasures are not always priceless for their value but for the pure excitement of their discovery. We know in our hearts that a true junker does not need to be an interior designer, antique dealer or even have a big budget to enjoy the spirit of collecting. The thrill of the hunt can be shared by everyone.

It is always junking season for us, and over the years we have become junk-obsessed with collecting what we affectionately call Flea Market Fidos. From straw-stuffed strays and paint-by-number pooches, to first edition breed reads and fetchingly framed etchings, Flea Market Fidos are a loveable litter of irresistible collectibles made up of mixed breeds and pure pedigrees alike.

Dogs have been a celebrated centerpiece in art and crafts for centuries. The history of their unconditional love and loyalty has been adoringly documented in everything from sporting hound paintings and working dog drawings, to pampered pup portraits and delicately detailed Fido figurines. These early wag-worthy works gave way to some kitschier collectibles (think souvenir cedar boxes and canine coasters).

Our fascination with Flea Market Fidos began with the gift of a Bakelite terrier pin from Grandma Emma and the purchase of a

pup
pals
dog and
devotees
forever

Clockwise from top:
A backyard sprinkler
snap of Barri and her
first dog, Fluffy, a
kick-line of canines
dance across Barri's
first flea market find
—a pillow for her daughter
Emma's nursery, Marie
showing off her poodle,
Pepe and a 1940s Bakelite
pin made for Grandmother
Emma by Marie's dad, Carl.

14ᵉ Arr!
PLACE
DE LA PORTE
DE VANVES

FRENCH FRIES
$1.75

PLEASE
HAVE
HAND
STAMPED

junk bonding
Our "philosoflea"?
Life is a never-
ending search for
Fidos and fries.

Opposite page:
A reunited pair
of chippy chalkware
dogs—one found
in a Chicago
junk shop, her
matching mate at a
Connecticut flea.

mym

hand-embroidered dancing dog pillow for baby Emma. These tiny treasures set off a Fido frenzy and our canine collections began to multiply weekly (at least that is what our husbands would have you believe!).

As self proclaimed pup collecting pros, we have admired auction house hounds (like pricey paintings and bronze finished bookends), but it's the striking strays that always win their place in our hearts and homes. These "junk dogs" are the never-second-best, simply secondhand fellas who are wonderfully well worn and irresistible.

Come along on a junking jaunt with Flea Market Fidos where we celebrate our doggone favorite canine collectible categories with hundreds of inspiring Fido photographs. We know our collected secrets, successes, tips and ideas for defining and reinventing our "ruff" discoveries will be all you need to get going.

Delve into delicious tidbits of found hound history, explore inventive ideas for collecting and displaying Fido finds and get up and go with our Go Fetch resource guide of secret sources. Whether celebrating a favorite breed, starting a little litter or adding to a hundred hound collection, *Flea Market Fidos* is sure to be a pet favorite—no bones about it.

puppy
love

heirlooms

clothing

toys

nursery

Previous pages:
A tower of terrier
blocks stack up
as sweet reminders
of simpler times.

This page: Dog
decorated treasures
for the nursery
(this one is great
for tucking away
Q-tips) are as
one-of-a-kind as a
new bundle of joy.

Opposite page: A tiny
trio of "ruff" and
ready rattles.

for centuries, dogs have been regarded as honorary family members, playful playmates and loyal protectors. Their special place in the home has been lovingly documented over time with furry faced images and icons decorating both practical and playful items for children. The very presence of a dog on a toy or baby accessory adds a warm touch to even the most everyday items.

When introduced to Flea Market Fidos while still pups—with a brood of breeds bedecking their nursery—little ones quickly become doggie devotees themselves. Watch their happy hound collections grow over the years as they begin collecting pup pieces of their own.

Puppy Love collectibles include scrapbooks, vintage quilts, and novel nursery items. Each dog decorated hope chest hand-me-down is sure to become an instant heirloom—and the "don't touch" rule for these collectibles is never needed because Flea Market Fidos are always begging to be held.

the welcoming of a child into the world calls for a vintage keepsake. A present from the past is sure to stand out among the usual bundle of baby fare bestowed upon a newborn, especially if it is something punctuated with a pup.

Search for gifts that can be both memorable and useful. Look for items like a never used 1940s Scottie scrapbook, a sterling spaniel rattle, or a hand-painted celluloid comb and brush set. These one-of-a-kind finds can often be had for a song and will certainly win the blue ribbon for most prized offering. Friends are sure to love the distinguishing appeal of a vintage baby gift that arrives bundled with a bit of history.

There is great joy in discovering a Puppy Love find. From one baby to the next, these items will fold perfectly into the heritage of a new family— now that's a true dog rescue for sure! Take care of these baby treasures and they'll live on as part of the family tree for generations to come.

Left: Fill a
newborn's nursery
with a litter
of darling dogs
like this Scottie
scrapbook or
(opposite) make
"groom" for a
decal decked comb
and brush set.

We spied this snuggly find at the Grayslake Antique and Collectibles Market in Illinois.

snakes and snails and puppy dog tails

Made of silver, this Parisian pooch rattle was rescued from a French flea market. It was tucked away for the imminent arrival of little Miss Moss.

woof woof
wearables

Whether peeking
out of pockets
or borrowing room
on a bib, Flea
Market Fido
wearables are little
works of art.

we're always on the hunt for Flea Market Fido's on handmade children's clothing. Those that stand the test of time are certainly a rare breed and finding them in mint condition is a testament to the quality of Old World textiles and to the loving care of the crafter.

Special pieces to look for include those with free-hand embroideries, knitted details and hand-cut appliqués. Hand-painted hangers are an equally prized find.

Lucky canine collectors may come upon the perfect size for a favorite child (or for their doll), but size rarely matters when stumbling upon a find. Miniature doll clothes make for chic little gift toppers, while other clothing collectibles can be framed and hung to admire.

Opposite page: A dog embroidered felt topper, a linen bib with Scottie at the red-y and a patriotic pup-pocket on a cozy sweater are sure to be layette favorites.

Right: A hand-painted "hang up" will give any child's closet real hanger appeal.

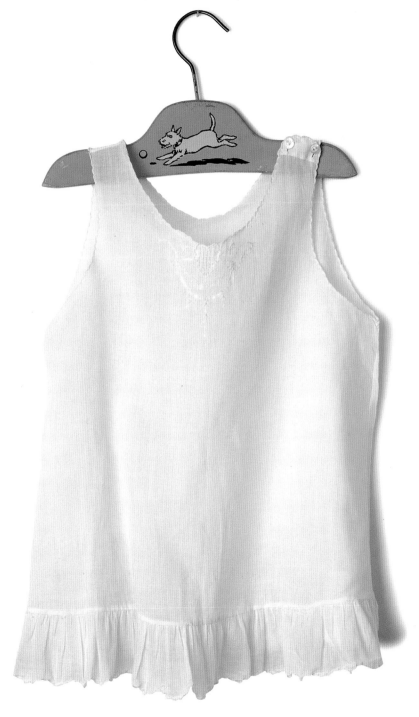

birth
of an idea

marie, stephen & twiggy
are thrilled to announce
the arrival of
the oh-so delicious

miss maisy hazel moss

july 26th, 2001
1:46 p.m.
7 pounds 12 ounces
20 inches

a very important announcement

The birth of Marie's daughter Maisy was destined to be documented with a fetching graphic. This image was borrowed from a vintage children's stationary set and printed on paper luggage tags.

celebrate the birth of baby with vintage pup announcements that are as special as a newborn. Shop flea markets and antique shops for growlingly great graphics, then enlist the help of the local printer or copy shop with a newborn's vitals in tow. Darling dog designs and drawings also make for bow WOW wonderful thank you notes, gift cards and library labels for a nursery.

pooch party

barri's daughter emma's dog-themed birthday get-together began with a stack of blank 1940s vintage advertising cards. A quick stamp of the details gathered her guests for mini hot dog hors d'oeuvres and a make believe Westminster showing of stuffed dogs. The party ended with Westie topped cupcakes and take home doggie bags filled with old time carnival prizes and charms. It was a howling success.

what to fetch for the fete?
Puppy particulars include flea-found cupcake toppers, new-but-old plastic poodle prizes and vintage advertising cards.

THREE DOZEN
BIRTHDAY CANDLES
BY
Master Craft

A KOPPERS product

2283 39

PETS FOR BABY

A REAL CLOTH BOOK

playdate with a past

set out on a junking jaunt and see pups take their place on everything from records and paint sets to picture puzzles and doll furniture.

Children and adults alike will be inspired by the very charm and simplicity of old fashioned favorites—a trip down the aisle of today's toy stores would never turn up such treasures. Hunt for flea finds that bring back memories of childhood and pass along the tradition. They just don't make 'em like they used to!

Above: A cloth book is a playful mate for baby.

Opposite page: Playroom finds include a dolly's highchair, pristine paintbox, poodle pretty cradle and an old-time tune.

"Little Miss"

Kiddie Set

Necklace and Bracelet and Brooch Set

This set set trio for the "Little Miss" was a rare find.

puttin' on the dog

these wearable waggers are a rare breed. Searching for them at the flea market reminds us of discovering treasures in grandma's jewelry box or in a family hope chest. We've learned to dig deep for these perfectly pretty pups who are often found hiding among the mix of tossed out trinkets. Look for pristinely packaged pups at local auctions where they are sometimes found in dead stock dozens.

Clockwise from above left: Who knew? A Parisian poodle in blue! This chic clip was brought home from a French flea. We snapped up this pup filled purse of plastic barrettes by Goody at a local tag sale. We grabbed this girly pair out from under a jumble of jewels.

doggie digs

why run with the pack when it comes to design? Create a dog friendly nursery or children's room with practical pup finds like hand-hooked rugs and chalkware poodle lamps. Happy 1940s and 50s graphics like poodles and Scotties can be playful companions when welcomed in to nestle in the nursery.

a little squirt

You won't have to spend your child's savings decorating their nursery or room with junk dog finds. We made a dash for the splash and took home this pair of wood cutouts for ten dollars!

just hanging
around

dog
d

wag-worthy walls

A mixed breed of
flea market finds
becomes wall art
when hiply clipped
in a doggie display.
Glue clothespins
across a painted
board or simply
clip them clothes-
line style along
the wall with some
twine. Create an
ever changing
gallery of mixed
media mutts by
searching for
pup items like
flashcards, fabric
swatches, greeting
cards and photos.

framing fido

Everyday items like sewing accessories

and book covers can be elevated to little

works of art when simply displayed inside a

frame. Collect a mixed bag of perfectly

cute canines like button cards, old book

jackets, and charms, or cover a child's walls

with one frame-worthy collectible category

for a whimsical display.

in the doghouse

boxes

doorstops

linens

needlepoint

games

Previous pages: The welcoming wag of a terrier doorknocker is stamped "England". We have uncovered other breeds of this somewhat elusive collectible.

This page & opposite: It is pillow talk in pairs for a Scottie embroidered cushion and terriers atop a peach satin pick.

pups with a purpose head home from the flea ready to lend a paw with decorating and everyday tasks. These eager to please homebodies have a way of making daily chores seem entertaining and playing house a breeze.

Our favorite decorative do-gooders are from the 1940s and 50s and include puppy potholders, terrier textiles and cocktail coasters. A bit harder to find, but worth the hunt, are household hounds like doorknockers, game boards, hand-hooked rugs and fireplace accessories.

These working dog collectibles are always on the clock. Whether cozying up on a comfy chair, propping open a porch door or keeping clutter at bay, these in the doghouse doggies want in on the action.

every dog has his day job

tidy up with handsome hounds that get the job done. A fireplace Fido helps sweep cinders while a bounty of boxes will strategically store life's little trinkets and treasures.

Atlantic City, N. J.

Opposite page: He might look like
a lounger but this fireside friend
is always on call. Marked
"Marutomoware, made in Japan,"
this sweeper is a keeper.

This page: A breed of "boxers"
from the 1920s to 50s were designed to
stash sewing supplies, cigars and matches.
Some simply served as souvenirs.

game boys

feel like puttin' on the dog?

Invite "Fred and Ethel" over for a retro Rover soiree! Fill out the doggone details on 1950s party invitations, then start planning an old fashioned game night.

Set the mood with cocktail coasters and kitschy party fare (please pass the treats!), then break out the bridge cards and get set for a fetching affair.

This page: A bottom-of-the-junk pile puzzle is painterly when placed together.

Opposite page (clockwise from bottom): This backgammon set was a $40 score (complete with Bakelite game pieces), send friends retro invites— this pack of ten was a $2 junk store find, serve up a vintage vibe with easy to find at the flea canine coasters, this sporty deck was a deal for $6.

welcome waggin'

cast iron canines have been decking doorstops for almost a century. Victorians gave the doorstop its decorative status, casting these heavy hounds into the spotlight. The Hubley Manufacturing Company is one of the most popular United States labels in this category, having cast iron into dutiful dogs from about 1910 to 1940. On the hunt for a Hubley? Look for numbered notations on their creations as this company did not use their name as markings. Some collectors are as sold on the mold of these stand-up finds as the doorstops themselves.

a stand up guy

Think it's a Hubley? This unmarked Boston Terrier keeps his owner, Nancy Powers, guessing about his identity.

Opposite page: There was a nationwide casting call for dog doorstops from the 1930s to 50s. Size, paint condition and pose are all factors in determining their weighty worth in today's market.

canine
cutouts

these wood shop wonders were often used to handle house numbers or to guard the garden gate. Consider previously painted pups that can be easily repainted and stenciled, or hunt for a clean slated canine in need of some numbering.

Other ideas for these outsiders include inscribing a family name, painting a shingle for a shop sign or assigning them a doggie directive ("please don't eat the daisies!").

This page: A house broken Scottie addresses the idea.

Opposite page: His numbers? A ten dollar stick-on price tag at a flea.

2948

hound
sweet
hound

cookin' canines

dog-decked kitchen kitsch will magically make even the most mundane chores seem fun. A well-stocked kitchen is one that includes a pinch of terrier textiles, a dash of pup potholders and a taste of Scottie shakers.

Little linens from the 1940s and 50s were the perfect canvas for showing off a homemaker's cross-stitch and embroidery talents.   Search for these or store bought prints and patterns that are just as fun to keep in the cupboard. While a single tattered towel may have strayed from its set, a collection of mixed-breeds is always a treat to have at the table.

needle
pointers

many vintage needlepoint works can be found sporting dogs at center stage. In recent years this age-old craft has gained new-found attention along with higher price tags. Finished finds include plump pillows, decorative doorstops and framed Fidos. Stumble upon someone's unfinished handiwork at a yard sale? Consider scooping it up and taking it home for a crafty reinvention.

in stitches

This page: Two needlepoint dogs are at home on wooden wedge doorstops. Smaller samplings are well suited for framing.

Opposite page: We stumbled upon this finished find for three dollars at a Chappaqua, New York tag sale.

under foot

Two black Labs lounge about an early American hand-hooked find (1920-1940). This wool rug was found in "very good" condition and priced at $375 at a Connecticut flea market. The dealer, Susan Goldsweig of Sage Antiques, finds that customers are often so delighted to discover their breed on a rug that they hang them up as works of art.

getting
hooked

crafting and creating hand-hooked rugs that showed off the family pet was a popular mid-19th century pastime. Put to work warming a bare floor, these colorful canines spent years of service underfoot, making an underused underdog hard to find. While a dog rug found in fair condition might be tagged anywhere from forty to a few hundred dollars, a barely worn Rover rug can fetch up to $2,500. While these are good guidlines to hunt by, the true value of these handmade finds lies as much in the breed it bears, as

pup art

drawings

artists

gallery

outsider art

Previous pages:
This paint by
number terrier is a
study in kitsch.

This page: We
found this guy
hunting for a new
owner at a Wisconsin,
flea market. This
outsider oil
painting was
framed and ready
for a cozy
spot in the den.

Opposite page:
A well-rounded
Rover print
was found at a
Connecticut
flea market.

dogs have long been celebrated subjects of the art world. These framed Fidos help to mark the lineage of particular breeds or portray their prowess on the hunt. From refined oil paintings to studied drawings (and even paint-by-number canvases), the dog continues to inspire artists as a faithful subject.

There are three breeds of pup art patrons – the purely purebred fan who collects ancestral renderings, the sporting dog devotee who fetches finds of the field and the pet-setter who simply can't resist a furry face. Whether searching for a Dandie Dinmont drawing, hunting for a canine canvas or uncovering a matted mixed breed, pup art collectors of all kinds are simply "hung-up" on finding a frame-worthy Fido.

Be a resourceful retriever—this hound-hungry bunch is a breed who will always be begging for more. Savvy pup art prowlers go beyond the flea and surf for online auction offerings or sniff out pup art dealers.

fetch a sketch

while an original drawing by a noteworthy dog artist might beg for more than a doggie dime or two, the signature style of their works can be found on the market with a keen eye and a bit of research.

At the high end are limited edition offerings by artists like Lucy Dawson, Marguerite Kirmse and Morgan Dennis. While flea market folklore regales us with stories of one dollar Dennis drawings discovered between the pages of dusty portfolios, the determined pup art collector is more likely to find one professionally framed and matted and selling for a few hundred dollars by a print dealer.

Framed reprints certainly make the fetch-factor less intimidating and up the odds of landing a Scottie study by dog-lover Dawson. Most reprints are copies of the artists' illustrations commissioned for books, magazines and advertisements but are loved for their endearing images all the same.

french fidos

This page and opposite: We were drawn to these two scruffy Frenchmen found unframed at a Paris antique shop.

i love
lucy dawson

These portraits of "Binkie" (this page) and "Creenagh" (far right) are from Dawson's book *Dogs As I See Them*. This portrait of a Maltese at rest (above right) is from her book *Dogs Rough and Smooth*.

who knew
that the
Mac moniker
was
Lucy Dawson
in disguise?

lucy dawson (1877-1958) Dawson's tail-wagging work began in her forties. The London elite commissioned Dawson to draw their pets' portraits, giving her access to "best-in-breed" models who "sat" for drawings used for illustrations and reproduction.

Dawson sometimes signed her work "Mac"—a moniker she used for less prestigious projects like her *Tailwagger* series of postcards commissioned by Valentine & Sons, Limited.

The author's first book, *Dogs As I See Them*, was a compilation of her dog portraits from English and American periodicals (Collins, London 1936 and Grosset & Dunlop, New York 1937). It included 22 color illustrations, pencil drawings, and her handwritten anecdotes about the personalities of the pups that posed for her. Her signature style is recognized by the combination of pastels, charcoal and pencil.

Three Rascals

kurt meyer-eberhard (1895-1977)

An early Meyer-Eberhardt depicts a trio of terriers (at left) and is entitled *Three Rascals*. This German-born artist was smitten with pups but dabbled beyond dogs in other animal etchings. His original plates are owned by the city of Munich and hand-printed color engravings continue to be printed today by the very same printer who employs the process used by the artist himself. Today, Meyer-Eberhardt restrikes are signed and authorized by his estate.

marguerite kirmse (1885-1954)

Known mostly for her etchings, the English-born Kirmse spent the 1930s in America where her prints and drawings of dogs, particularly Scotties, gained popularity and a large following. She purchased and maintained a large farm and kennel in Connecticut where she bred terriers and field dogs—the personality of her subjects was captured in her art by catching them in action. Kirmse illustrated many books but *Dogs*, a limited edition collectible (Derrydale Press, Lanham, Maryland, 1930), contains an original etching of a Scottie entitled *Hello There!* that can range in price from $1,200 to $2,000.

Right: A reprint of a Kirmse etching entitled *Up for Inspection* (1929).

Opposite page: This framed Morgan Dennis print was a Pennsylvania flea find.

morgan dennis (1892-1960) While his name might not be tip-of-the-tongue for some, his work as the creator of Blackie and Scottie, the memorable stars of the Black & White Scotch Whiskey ads, is widely known and highly regarded. His book and magazine illustrations are favorites among pup art collectors.

gladys emerson cook (1899-1976) This American artist specialized in drawing and painting animals. Her book, *All Breeds, All Champions, A Book of Dogs* (Harper & Row, New York 1962) features over one hundred pup portraits, including everything from sporting pointers to toy Maltese. This great Scot is a pencil perfect example of Cook's talent for capturing the personality of a posing pooch.

fancy fidos

seriously secord

Two of William Secord's favorite oil paintings.

Above: *A Dog Looking Out of a Kennel* (1837) by Sir Edwin Henry Landseer (English, 1802-1873). Right: *Italian Greyhound* (1866) by Rosa Bonheur (French, 1822-1899).

Canine connoisseurs head straight to the one-of-its-kind William Secord Gallery on Manhattan's Upper East Side for the serious stuff. Others pop in to peek at Secord's extensive collection of dog art and collectibles or to preview the newest exhibit.

Secord is known worldwide as the absolute authority on the dog in art. His passion lies in nineteenth-and early twentieth-century antique paintings and he has written several books on the subject including *Dog Painting, 1840 - 1940, a Social History of the Dog in Art* (Antique Collectors' Club Limited, Woodbridge, Suffolk, England 1992). He was the founding director of the Dog Museum of America (a St. Louis must-see!) until he opened his gallery in 1990, and has been a national board member of Directors of the ASPCA since 1997.

His favorite find-in-the-ruff? An F. T. Daws painting of a Wire-Haired Fox Terrier for $75 (worth over $2,500!) found in a Canadian antique store. His dog art mantra? "Buy the best art your budget will allow and buy only what you love—end of story!"

hanging up

pups d'resistance

A collection of
tail-waggin' wall-
flowers keep each
other company.

want to show off blue ribbon finds? Why not display a playful pup art collection by hanging a large print at center and layering on the litter of art as it arrives home from the flea market. This mixed medium of mixed breeds is sure to gain showcase status when hung as a collection. If space is at a premium, try tucking finds into bookshelf nooks, layering them along base moldings or propping them up on the windowsill. Keep prints and paintings away from direct sunlight or consider framing a find in a museum quality matte and UV protective glass.

We found that a quick chat with the dealer might turn up some interesting info about a pup art purchase. Jot the information on the back of a find for safe keeping.

This page: An artful oil on a backyard pal.

Opposite page: A walk in the park painting bought in a Red Bank, New Jersey, antique store for $9.

pet project

we have art class upstarts and Sunday painters to thank for some of the most lovable pup art on the market. These amateur odes to pet pals are often signed and are truly one-of-a-kind. Whether scooped up at the flea for a take on a terrier or admired at an estate sale for a modeling Maltese, these crafty collectibles are true strokes of genius. Now go outside.

This page: An
Airedale in acrylic
strikes a pose by "JT."

Opposite page: A
study by "Ellen
Broomfield" was a $30
find at a New York City
flea market.

brushing up on breeds

This page: This pup on a pedestal looks for a buyer.

Opposite page (clockwise from top left): A peely pup and three paint-by-number neighbors: A crafty Collie, "Victor Pollard's" pups and a prim Poodle.

ruff
stuff

fabric

labels

poodles

minis

Previous pages:
A stand-up pup found
at an online auction.

This page: A German
Shepherd says "cheese."

Opposite page:
It's Monsieur Mutt
straight from a Parisian
marche aux puces.

collectors of all ages find it hard to resist the happily wagging "take-me-home" tail of a stuffed stray. Some are prized for their pedigree (is he wearing his original dog tags?), while others are collected for their cuddling cachet. Whether it's the tattered tuft of a terrier's coat or the glossy glance of a button eye, these coy canines will quickly turn a single Fido find into a mutt menagerie.

Whether collecting one or 101, every day is a stuffed dog soiree when calling these furry Fidos friends. These low maintenance, allergy free friends require little grooming and never need a walk. Plenty more than playthings, this breed deserves all-day adoring. Line them up dog show style on a shelf or give them a Rover roost upon a comfy chair and these little guys will instantly feel like part of the family.

a six-pack
A team of
tattered
terriers
rescued from
fleas around
the world.

puppy patterns
Flowery Fidos
found at fleas
and Scottie
cutouts from
an online auction.

fabric
fidos

Printed and patterned pups were crafty canines made from simple sewing patterns of the 1940s and 50s. Home Economics classes had students in stitches, while sewing up Scottie cutouts that first made the grade, then went home to curl up as pillows and play pals.

tag you're it!

the label conscious collector plays tag at the flea market searching for names like Steiff, Gund Manufacturing Company and R. Dakin & Company. These tell-tale tickets to collectibility serve up value and a peek at a stuffed pal's pedigree.

Stumble upon a Steiff? Some of these collectible canines are still manufactured today but it is the sight of a vintage Steiff dog at a tag or estate sale that guarantees panting on the part of most Flea Market Fido collectors.

Seamstress Margarete Steiff's "Felt Toy Company" opened for business in 1880. She found sweet success with her handmade menagerie and began tagging her animals with the signature "button-in-ear" to assure collectors they were purchasing a stuffed Steiff and not a copycat (or dog, or bear or bunny!).

pups with a pedigree

Top left: Gund's Pepe the Airedale was part of the Blue Ribbon Pups Group, 1969. We found him at Brimfield for $12.

Top right: A Dakin-labeled dog is also quite collectible. This California cutie was brought home for $9 from the Rose Bowl Flea Market.

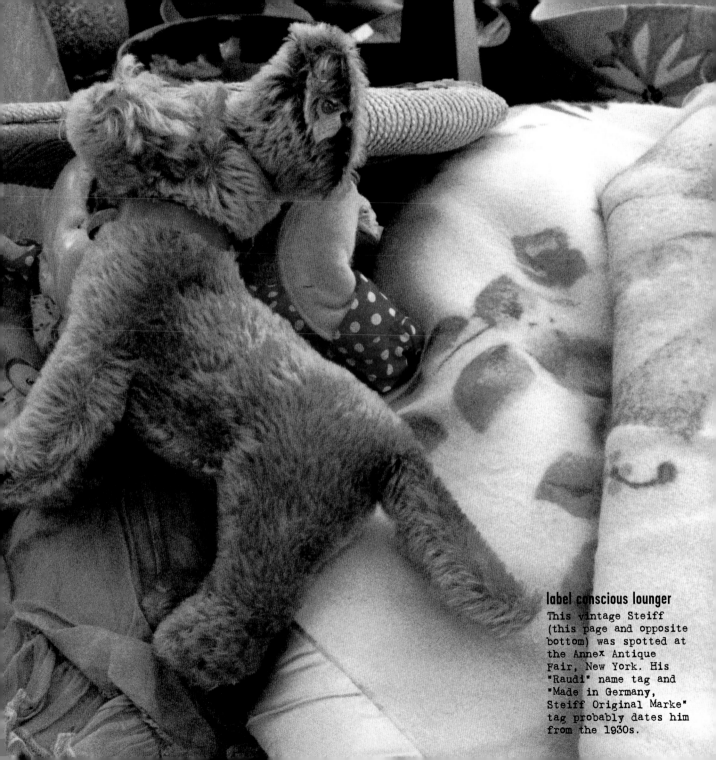

label conscious lounger

This vintage Steiff (this page and opposite bottom) was spotted at the Annex Antique Fair, New York. His "Raudi" name tag and "Made in Germany, Steiff Original Marke" tag probably dates him from the 1930s.

oodles of poodles

poodles are one of the most adored breeds among flea market finders, with stuffed Standards (and Miniatures and Toys!) serving as standouts. So fashionably French (they are the official dogs of France), their famously delightful dispositions guaranteed them top spots as perfectly pleasing poupées.

Tiny terriers **often** turn up at flea markets **tucked**

away in the bottom of **boxes** or teetering atop

old armoires. A shy bunch, these diminutive

doggies are **nevertheless** a hearty breed,

surviving **decades** spent **curled up** inside

sewing satchels and **overstuffed** doll trunks.

pup parade

A Lilliputian
line-up of
our favorite
flea-sized Fidos.

paper
trained

desk accessories

books

photographs

greeting cards

gift wrap

playing cards

great scot!

Don't be surprised to find a stray playing card without his pack curled up inside a box of flea market junk. These deck free dogs can often be brought home for less than a buck. What to do with a solitaire? (right) Treat your new pal to work of art status by showing him off in a vintage frame.

Previous pages: A metal flip-top notepad keeper from the 40s was discovered at an on-line auction for $24.

doesn't every dog owner dream of a paper trained pup? It is the irresistible images and most often affordable price tags that make Flea Market Fido paper treats the perfect category for kicking off a canine collection. Just follow the paper trail of these everyday items that include everything from black and white snapshots and playing cards to gift wrap and books.

While dog-bedecked ephemera might be considered the more delicate of the breeds, these collectible treasures have hung tight to their hardiness, managing to survive dog decades with only a few tattered corners here and there.

Often hidden between the pages of books or at the bottom of a beat up box, these paper pieces of the past can easily be overlooked but are well worth the hunt. We love when dog days are dated and documented on the flip side of photos and in the seams of scrapbooks—all offering a glimpse of a pup's past.

working dogs

the next assignment? Look for practical desk top dogs to help get the job done. For the collector who likes pups with a purpose, these utilitarian items will easily earn their keep as office assistants. When space for collectibles is hard to find, this breed will supply its own work environment atop a desk or tucked away in a drawer.

Left: This wooden perpetual calendar with all of its original pieces was found at a Paris flea market for $38.

Above: A ceramic Scottie tape dispenser has its original sticker intact and is marked "Takahashi San Francisco, Made in Japan."

Vendredi Octobre 29

90

case
in point

We gave non-smoking status to these hers and hers metal cigarette cases by turning them into business card holders. Scottie cases like these became all the rage in the 1930s when women began carrying them to weekly card games.

Above: *Grabby Pup* by Nancy Raymond, illustrated by
Dirk (Fideler Company, Grand Rapids, Michigan, 1945),
Where are you? by Sam See, illustrated Frank
Leiberman (Simon and Schuster, New York, 1941).
The Very Little Dog by Grace Skaar (A Young Scott
Book, U.S.A. 1949), *Poker Dog* by Sarah Derman,
illustrated by Jack Boyd (Benefic Press Chicago,
Illinois, 1958).

Opposite page: *Dogs as I See Them* by Lucy Dawson
(Grosset & Dunlap, New York, 1937), *Dogs, Paintings
and Stories* (Saalfield Publishing, Akron, Ohio, 1932)
and *Around the World with Children and Dogs* by
Diana Thorne (McLoughlin Bros. Inc. Springfield,
Massachusetts, 1940).

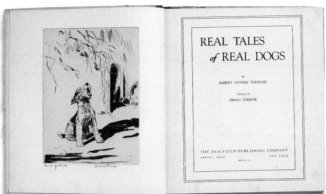

Real Tales
of Real Dogs
written by
Albert Payson
Terhune,
illustrated
by Diana Thorne
was one in
a series of
collaborations by
the pair
(Saalfied
Publishing Co.,
Akron, Ohio, 1935).

breed
reads

dog tales are a popular category among book collectors and dealers who look for everything from well-known authors and illustrators to clever titles and favorite breeds. Those flea-goers with a trained eye have been known to roll over and beg for a first edition illustrated by Cecil Aldin or a hard to find copy of a Diana Thorne. Others may be thrilled to find castoff treasures like the loose pages of dog drawings from children's books or dog-eared pet stories.

Many vintage children's books gave center stage to playful dogs and their adventures. Lighthearted copy, sweet illustrations and little life lessons make these breed reads impossible to leave behind.

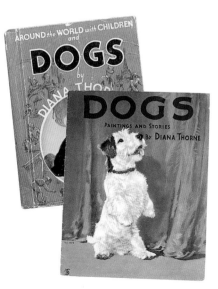

breed
read
rules

- First edition books can be worth fifty to one hundred percent more with dust jackets intact.

- A "breaker" is the term used for a book that is beyond repair but its illustrations can still be of value.

- Vintage editions by authors Albert Payson Terhune, Jim Kjelgaard and Jack London are some of the most noteworthy of dog books.

- Ex-library books and book club editions have limited value in the resale market.

This page: Coming upon a picnic basket stuffed with readable treats at a swap meet has us crossing our paws for a rare find.

Opposite page: Words worth a library shelf are titles that speak for themselves.

fidos
on film

whether found loose or taped inside photo albums, black and white snapshots featuring family dogs are an endearing and nostalgic addition to a Flea Market Fido collection. Our favorite finds are impromptu portraits from the 1930s to 50s shot by dog owners (and amateur photographers!) in backyards and front porches the world over—who better to capture the spirit and personality of these furry family members than their masters?

dog dish
Display a
collection of
loose dog
photos in
a vintage
silver compote
for hands-on
admiring.

all animals
are equal,
but some
are more equal
than others.
—George Orwell

pen pals

vintage greeting card graphics and sappy salutations are what make these mailable mementos gifts unto themselves. We think it's the dog tricks that make these cards worth saving and sending like a moveable tail or an interesting finish (glitter, feathers and felt are favorites). Good wishes for every big and little occasion (holiday greetings for the postman!) are what make the unsigned greeting card perhaps the most elusive breed of Fido ephemera. Signed, sealed and delightful.

Dog-adorned greetings were most charming from the 1920s to 60s.

signed finds

don't leave behind a great vintage card just because it has been signed inside. Simply recycle these bygone greetings by cutting off the card's front cover and adding a punched hole and some ribbon (or a little charm or two) for one-of-a-kind gift tags and party invitations.

Greet the **new year**
with a resolution to
recycle by sending
salvaged **cards** to
old acquaintances.

wrap
happy

happiness is discovering a

stack of unused vintage wrapping paper decorated with dogs. Total exhilaration can occur when matching stickers—like the one above—appear in the pile. Treat a special gift to these trimming treasures or use a favorite sheet as a matte for a photograph in a frame or to transform the cover of a cookbook or journal. Opposite page: This 1950s wrapping paper full of resting Rovers is marked "A Commodore Original, Made in U.S.A."

playing with
a full deck

the playing card has been dealing out good times for over 600 years. In England and the United States, decorated packs were a mid-19th-century innovation with printers and designers wild for this new canvas. While some Fido fans simply revel in a good game of bridge, others count themselves as either single card or full deck collectors.

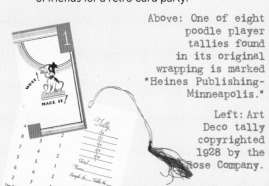

tally tips

card party

Slip one-off cards into a scrapbook or make the unvarnished "no-slip" variety into business cards with a personalized rubber stamp or felt-tip marker.

Don't be surprised to find 1930s to 1950s.rare singles for as much as $12 each, though we found these for a song.

Tallies were often sold to match playing card decks and bridge party themes. Teach an old dog new tricks by scooping up tally singles to use as nifty gift tags. Got lucky and discovered a complete set in its original wrap? It might be time to host a full house of friends for a retro card party!

Above: One of eight poodle player tallies found in its original wrapping is marked "Heines Publishing-Minneapolis."

Left: Art Deco tally copyrighted 1928 by the Rose Company.

real
tails

friend

companion

pal

protector

Previous pages:
We met Flossie
at the Sandwich
Antiques Market
in Sandwich,
Illinois.

table for deux
marche aux puces
porte de vanves, france

the most irresistible Flea Market Fidos are the trusty companions who accompany their owners on junking journeys. These road trip Rovers make their way across the country in junk filled trucks, sniffing out the next opportunity to show off their salesdog skills. From the Pasadena Rose Bowl to Brimfield's acres of antiques, this pedigree of pooch uses its tail wagging skills to bark for a bite and move the merchandise.

This breed is as dedicated as the dealers themselves. From establishing booth boundaries to standing guard of the goods, their only distraction is the scent of home cooked goodies being served up in fairground kitchens.

"you break it, you buy it"
marche aux puces
porte de vanves, france

suzy q.
kane county flea market
st. charles, illinois

zoe
the garage antiques and collectibles market
new york, new york

lizzie
annex antique fair flea market
new york, new york

annie III
shop dog
lake geneva, wisconsin

tippy
sandwich antiques market
sandwich, illinois

a scratch player
marche aux puces
porte de vanves, france

coco
kane county flea market
st. charles, illinois

clothes call
marche aux puces
porte de vanves, france

bear
grayslake antique
and collectibles market
grayslake, illinois

nap attack
brimfield antiques market
brimfield, massachussets

on guard
sandwich antiques market
sandwich, illinois

dog tired
puces de st-owen
port de cliqnancourt, france

zima
kane county flea market
st. charles, illinois

bargain hunter
marche aux puces
porte de vanves, france

ricardo bingo
kane county flea market
st. charles, illinois

nicky paws
sandwich antiques market
sandwich, illinois

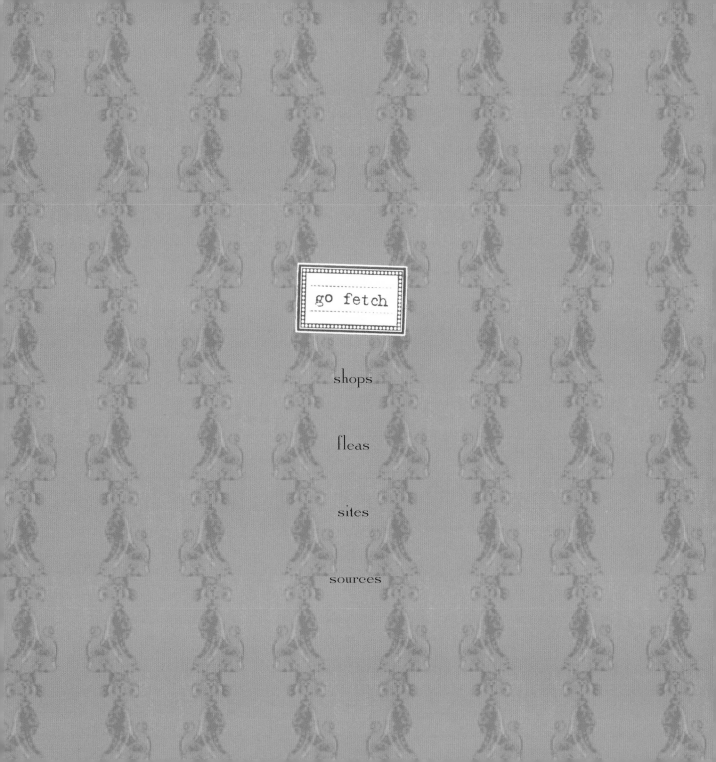

go fetch

shops

fleas

sites

sources

Ready to
retrieve a litter
or a lot?
Pay a visit
to our
Flea Market Fido
friends who are
sure to be
stocked with
the most
fetching
dog finds and
info around.

pet shop

Antique Centre
2012 N. Scottsdale Road
Scottsdale, AZ 85257

**The Antiques Center
of Red Bank**
195B, 195 and
226 West Front Street
Red Bank, NJ 07701
732.741.5331
732.842.3393
732.842.4336

Antiques Emporium
70 West Main Street
Somerville, NJ 08876
908.231.8850

Antique Trove
2020 N. Scottsdale Road
Scottsdale, AZ 85257
480.947.6074
www.antiquetrove.com

Bittersweet Antiques
Debby Gorin
37 Main Street
Tarrytown, NY 10591
914.366.6292
and by appointment

**Brimfield Antiques
and Collectibles Show**
Route 20
Brimfield, MA 01010
413.245.3436
www.jandj-brimfield.com

Dog Treasures
(online shop)
1430 Manor Road
Coatesville, PA 19320
610.380.4953
www.dogtreasures.com

Dogma Antiques
Deborah White
914.242.3270
by appointment

The Four Paws Club
387 Bleecker Street
New York, NY 10014
212.367.8265
thefourpawsclub@earthlink.net

Heritage Trail Mall
410 Ridge Road
Wilmette, IL 60091
htmltd@ameritech.net
847.256.6208

Jackson Square Mall
112 East Burlington
LaGrange, IL 60525
708.352.4120

The Last Detail
Martin Greenstein
342 Lexington Avenue
Mt. Kisco, NY 10549
914.572.4132
mgkisco@aol.com

Lucie Favreau Antiques
1904 Notre-Dame West
H3J 1M6
Montreal, Canada
514.989.5117
www.lucie@favreauantiques.com

Point Pleasant Antique Emporium
Bay and Trenton Avenues
Point Pleasant Beach, NJ 08742
732.892.222

Point Pleasant Pavillion Antique Centre
608 Arnnold Avenue
Point Pleasant Beach, NJ 08742
732.899.6300

Nancy Powers Collectibles & Antiques
npowers@genevaonline.com
by appointment
and online auction

Sage Antiques
Susan Goldsweig
P.O. Box 144
Yonkers, NY 10710
914.912.3546
shows and by appointment

This Old Book
Kim and Matt Meyer
thisoldbook@anet-chi.com
out of print, collectible
and old books

Vintage Home
Rossana Fiore-Tranzillo
144 King Street
Chappaqua, NY 10514
914.238.3014

Uncle Fun
1338 West Belmont
Chicago, IL 60657
www.unclefunchicago.com
vintage toy collectibles

Michael Aldin Associates, Inc.
P.O. Box 131952
The Woodlands, TX 77393
936.273.9662
www.traditionalart.com
specializing in
Kurt Meyer-Eberhardt

Kay Lopata Fine Art
P.O. Box 233
Wycombe, PA 18980
215.598.0792
www.kaylopatafineart.com
gallery shows
and by appointment

The William Secord Gallery, Inc.
52 East 76th Street
New York, NY 10021
212.249.0075
1.877.249.DOGS
www.dogpainting.com
fine art and collectibles

Ann Arbor Antiques Market
Washtenaw
Farm Council Grounds
5055 Ann Arbor Saline Road
Ann Arbor, MI 48103
www.annarborantiques
market.com

Annex Antique Fair & Flea Market
Avenue of the Americas
(between 24th & 26th Streets)
New York, NY 10011
212.243.5343
212.243.7922 day of market

Antique Flea Market
Walworth County Fairgrounds
Highway 11
Elkhorn, WI 53121
262.723.5651

Cow Palace Antique & Collectible Show
2600 Geneva Avenue
Daily City, CA 94014
503.282.0877
www.palmerwirfs.com

Dupage County Flea Market
Dupage County Fairgrounds
2015 Manchester Road
Wheaton, IL 60187
630.668.6636
dupagefair@ameritech.net
www.dupagecountyfair.org

Elephant's Trunk Bazaar
Route 7 & I-84
New Milford, CT 06776
860.355.1448

The Garage Antiques & Collectibles
112 West 25th Street
(Avenue of the Americas & 7th Ave)
New York, NY 10002
212.647.0707
212.463.0200

Grayslake Antique and Collectibles Market
Lake County Fairgrounds
Route 120 & US45
Grayslake, IL 60130
715.526.9769
www.zurkoantiquetours.com

Kane County Antique Flea Market
Kane County Fairgrounds
Route 64 & Randall Road
St. Charles, IL 60174
630.377.2252
www.2.pair.com/kaneflea

Marche aux Puces
Porte de Vanves/Porte Didot
Avenue Georges
Lafenestre/Avenue Marc Sangnier
75014 Paris

The Pec Thing Antique Market
Winnebago County Fairgrounds
500 West 1st Street
Pecatonica, IL 61063
800.238.3587
pecthing@winnebago
countyfair.com
(Rover over to Rick and Linda
Gibson's booth)

Puces de St-Ouen
Porte de St-Ouen/Porte de
Clignancourt
75018 Paris

Renningers-Adamstown
2500 N. Reading Road
Denver, PA 17517
717.336.2177
www.renningers.com

Renningers-Kutztown
740 Noble Street
Kutztown, PA 19530
610.683.6848
www.renningers.com

Rose Bowl Flea Market
Rose Bowl Stadium
1001 Rose bowl Drive
Pasadena, CA 91103
323.560.SHOW
www.rgcshows.com

Sandwich Antiques Market
The Fairgrounds
State Route 34
Sandwich IL 60548
773.227.4464
815.786.3337 day of show
www.antiquemarkets.com

**Stormville Airport
Antique Show and
Flea Market**
Route 216
Stormville, NY 12582
845.221.6561

**Wolff's Outdoor
Flea Market**
Allstate Arena
Mannheim Road
(between Higgins Road &
Touny Avenue)
Rosemont, IL 60018
847.524.9590
www.wolffsfleamarket.com

surf dog

www.akc.org
American Kennel Club, Inc.

www.collectors.org
flea market directory

www.ebay.com
online auction site

www.maiasaura.com
books and canine collectibles

www.les-puces.com
French flea market site

www.sothebys.com
online auction house

www.whatsitworthtoyou.com
online appraisals

www.steiffusa.com
official Steiff website

www.gund.com
Gund Manufacturing
Company website

ruff resources

**The American
Kennel Club Library**
260 Madison Avenue
4th Floor
New York, NY 10016
212.696.8245
www.akc.org/insideakc
/depts/library.cfm

**The American
Kennel Club
Museum of the Dog**
1721 South Mason Road
St. Louis, MO 63131
314.821.3647
dogarts@aol.com

pup pages

**A Breed Apart
William Secord**
Antique Collectors' Club Limited
(Woodbridge, Suffolk England)

**Exploring the
Flea Markets of France**
Sandy Price
(Three Rivers Press, NY)

U.S. Flea Market Directory
Albert LaFarge
(St. Martin's Griffin, NY)

how much is that doggie in the window?

ADDITIONAL
DEALERS

←

Together we visit
every junk shop,
antique mall,
side-of-the-road
stop, yard sale
and web address
in search of Flea
Market Fidos.

ANTIQUE SHOW & FLEA
← FAIRGROUNDS ← MARKET

Thank
You
FOR
ATTENDING
YOUR FAIR

"YOURS FAITHFULLY."

A Lucy Dawson
Tailwagger postcard
from Valentine & Sons
Limited.

we wag our tails to...

Our editor and publisher, Leslie Stoker, for believing in a new breed and giving our FMF's a place to call home. Howard Reeves and Eric Himmel for putting our project into the right paws. Nicole Salzano for her "arf"-ful vision and never-ending pup patience. Kooks the cat, for putting up with the dogs. Nancy Cohen (and Violet) for cozying up to the project (and the boxes!) and guiding us through. To Kim Tyner, Caroline Enright and everyone at STC for their doggone help and support. Aimée Herring (and Charlie and Issy) for her pup portraiture and superb spackling talents. Nancy Powers (and Annie III and Rudy) for cheering us on, a country lunch and letting us borrow from her litter. William Secord and Galina Zhitomirsky for help with the fancy Fidos. Peter Embling for sniffing out the mystery of Mac. Ann Sergi at the American Kennel Club for help with the "ruff" research. Peter Fields for double-checking the doggie details. Gund for helping with the hound history. The friendly flea market dealers and their devoted dogs for letting us sniff around. Bart and Twiggy for their inspiration and loyalty.

barri thanks...

Eddie (boy, I l.l.a.m.f.), Emma for inheriting a love of vintage, Dad for always lending a paw, Danna for being proud of my new tricks and Mom for the "good grooming." My family—I love you more than the whole wide world. m. — here's to forever friends, fries and to following our flea dreams. Couldn't have done it without you! xo, b.

marie thanks...

STM for finding sausage sandwiches and understanding a girl's need to flea, Maisy and Mom for doing some junk bonding of your own, Jo-Mom for your flea market photo assisting, Marianne for laughing 'til we cry, Rosemary for rescuing my favorite Fido and Judy for her junkabilities. b. — for road trip therapy sessions, bubbly at cafe flores and a flea friendship that has taught me the value of life's little treasures. x, m.